CELEBRATE
HOLIDAYS

Celebrate St. Patrick's Day

Heather Miller

Members of a marching band from Pennsylvania march in a
St. Patrick's Day parade in Baltimore, Maryland.

Enslow Publishers, Inc.
40 Industrial Road
Box 398
Berkeley Heights, NJ 07922
USA
http://www.enslow.com

Library of Congress Cataloging-in-Publication Data

Miller, Heather.
   Celebrate St. Patrick's Day / Heather Miller.
      p. cm. — (Celebrate holidays)
   Includes bibliographical references and index.
   ISBN 0-7660-2581-0
      1. Saint Patrick's Day—Juvenile literature. I. Title: Celebrate
Saint Patrick's Day. II. Title. III. Series.
   GT4995.P3M55 2006
   394.262—dc22
                          2005028112

Printed in the United States of America

10 9 8 7 6 5 4 3 2 1

Illustration Credits: © 1999 Artville, LLC., p. 10; Associated Press, pp. 1, 42, 50, 70, 74, 80, 86; Associated Press, CP, p. 52; Associated Press, PAMPC PA, p. 78; Associated Press, The Press, p. 47; Corel Corporation, pp. 26, 83; Enslow Publishers, Inc., p. 15; © 2005 JupiterImages, pp. 4, 5, 7, 8, 11, 19, 23, 27, 32, 37, 41, 43, 54, 55, 56, 57, 60, 63, 68, 71; Courtesy of Mary O'Connor, pp. 65, 90.

Cover Illustration: Associated Press.

CONTENTS

St. Patrick's Miracles

It may seem strange for an infant to be credited with healing a blind man's eyesight, or for a young boy to turn ice into fire, but in the case of St. Patrick, these are only a few of the many miracles that legends have connected with this important saint.

Soon after he was born, Patrick was brought to a young blind man named Gornias to be baptized into the Christian faith. But when the time came for the baptism to be performed, there was no water to be found. Gornias took the hand of the baby into his own and made the sign of the cross over the ground where they stood. At that very moment, a stream of water broke through the earth. Gornias scooped the water into his hands and splashed it over his own face. After he did this, his blindness was miraculously cured. To add to the amazement of this miracle, legends say that even though Gornias had never seen the letters of the alphabet, he was able to read the words written in the order of baptism without error. This three-part miracle was the first of many marvels that this newborn, St. Patrick, would bring forth.[1]

As a young boy, the stories of miracles continued. While still a very small child, Patrick single-handedly saved his foster-mother's home from ruin by a flood.[2] While playing inside the house one day, a rush of water filled Patrick's home, doused the cooking fire, and sent the contents of his home bobbing on the water. Legends say Patrick climbed to a dry place then dipped his fingers into the water. The drips that fell from his fingertips turned into sparks. The sparks grew into hungry flames that quickly consumed the floodwaters.[3]

Another story involving fire tells of Patrick gathering an armload of icicles, then laying them at his foster-mother's feet. When she complained that dry sticks were needed to build a fire, Patrick placed the ice in the fireplace and blew across it. Miraculously, the ice burst into flames, just as if it were indeed a pile of dry twigs.[4]

The stories of miracles performed during Patrick's life followed him to his death. Some stories say that on the day St. Patrick died, the sun never set. For the next twelve days, hymns were sung throughout Ireland, and during those twelve days, the darkness of night never fell upon the land.[5]

Strange stories surround the death of St. Patrick.

Tales of strange happenings continued after St. Patrick was buried. Many people believe that those who disturbed the burial site of the saint have been cursed with bad luck. It has been said that when Patrick's remains were disrupted during the construction of a new church that was built on the land where he was buried, the church burst into flames.[6]

St. Patrick is honored in many places, like Tara, Ireland.

Although most people believe these legends are most likely fairy tales passed down through history by storytellers, one cannot deny their powerful message. St. Patrick was a man whose life is highly regarded by many people. Even today, the stories that tell of the life of St. Patrick are treasured tales that continue to be passed from generation to generation.

WESTERN EUROPE

Norwe

NORW

Atlantic Ocean

SCOTLAND

DENMARK

IRELAND

ENGLAND

NETHERLANDS

BELGIUM   GERMA

LUXEM

FRANCE

SWITZERLAND

PORTUGAL

SPAIN

ITAL

The History of
St. Patrick's Day

The history of Saint Patrick's life has often been disputed. There have been many discussions between historians who argue that some of the stories describing St. Patrick are more like fables than facts. The truth is that it is difficult to know. Early history was not carefully recorded, and in the case of Saint Patrick's life, there are many conflicting tales. For example, it is difficult for historians to agree on the year Saint Patrick was born. Various dates ranging from the years

A.D. 387 to 416 and beyond have been found in historical record books. His death, the time he arrived in Ireland, and even his name are more examples of some of the events and ideas in Saint Patrick's life that cannot be confirmed as facts.[1]

Kidnapped!

Over one thousand years ago, ships filled with men sailed across the Irish Sea[2] with plans to steal property and people. They landed on the shores of the British Isles, most likely near Wales. The groups of men were from Hibernia, the place we now call Ireland. When the Irish raiders landed in Wales, they attacked a large homestead filled with servants and expensive goods. The raiders stole valuable items and kidnapped some of the people that lived in the home, then threw their bound captives into a boat.[3] A teenage boy named Maewyn Succat was one of those captives.[4]

The sixteen-year-old prisoner was taken across the sea into Ireland and sold as a slave by the raiders who captured him. A man named Miliuc bought Succat and sentenced him to a life of hard labor. Succat was forced to work in the mountains as a shepherd watching over Miliuc's flocks of sheep.

Succat lived alone on mountainsides and in forests, tending the sheep as they grazed for food. Succat's life as a shepherd was difficult. He worked hard and slept in the rain and cold. Many nights Succat sat in the dark, frightened by the emptiness that surrounded him. During this lonely time, he began to develop a close relationship with God. He prayed during the day and through the night asking God for comfort and guidance.

Succat wrote his own story much later in life,

> . . . my spirit was moved so that [each] day I said from one up to a hundred prayers. . . . I used to stay out in the forests and on the mountain and I would wake up before daylight to pray in the snow, in icy coldness, in rain. . . . [5]

Many stories claim that Succat lived in the mountains with the sheep for over six years. During that time he had many mysterious dreams. One night, an angel spoke to Succat in a powerful dream that changed the course of his life. The angel told him to run away and escape to the sea where a ship would be waiting to take him home. Succat believed the dream was a message sent from God. He followed the angel's message and walked what some stories say was over two hundred miles to the coast of Ireland.[6]

When he finally reached the sea, Succat found a ship and crew preparing to set sail. Succat approached the group of men and asked if he could ride along on their journey. The men quickly said no. Succat left the men and prayed to God as he walked away from the ship. He explained his experience:

> . . . and before the prayer was finished I heard one of them shouting loudly after me: "Come quickly because the men are calling you."[7] Succat believed his prayers had been answered. He was invited to join the men on their voyage across the sea. Soon, he would be home.

The ship sailed east for three days.[8] Unfortunately, disaster struck Succat and the crew. Violent storms erupted at sea. Many stories say huge waves tossed and tore at the ship then sent it crashing into the rocky shore.

Once again, Succat was faced with hardship. He and the sailors found themselves stranded in a place far from civilization. He stayed with the sailors as they traveled across the country in search of the nearest village.

The group traveled for many weeks. The men became very tired and hungry. They had run out of food and were surrounded by nothing but barren

When they spotted a herd of wild pigs, the captain believed that God had answered Patrick's prayers.

land. Some of the men collapsed along the road and many of them began to lose hope.

Through all of his struggles, Succat never lost his hope or his faith in God. Once again, he called out to God and asked for help. Some legends state that during his prayer, a herd of wild pigs suddenly appeared on the road. Succat wrote his account of the story:

> . . . and behold, a herd of swine appeared on the road before our eyes, and they slew many of them, and remained there for two nights, and they were full of meat and well restored.[9]

The band of sailors did not know where the pigs had come from, but they were glad they had appeared. They stuffed their bellies with food and, with regained strength, were able to travel on. Succat's prayers seemed to have saved him yet again. After witnessing what appeared to be a miracle, some of the sailors began to believe in Succat's God. Succat explains his account of the story:

> And after this they gave the utmost thanks to God, and I was esteemed in their eyes, and from that day they had food abundantly.[10]

But bad luck soon found Succat again. As the group traveled on, they were attacked and imprisoned by a band of raiders. Although the history of this event is a bit unclear, Succat writes that he was not held captive long. While being held hostage, yet another voice spoke to Succat with a message from God. The voice explained to Succat that he would be held captive for only two months. Succat wrote: "So it happened. On the sixtieth night the Lord delivered me from their hands."[11]

Succat was set free.

Although he may not have known at the time, Succat was close to home. He set out to travel again. This time he was blessed with a constant supply of food, fire for cooking, and dry weather every day. On the tenth day of traveling, he came upon people. Finally, Succat's long, difficult journey was over. He was home.

He may have been glad to be home, but Succat felt a nagging urge to leave again. He felt God was calling him to do something, something very important. Succat prepared for a long journey and bid farewell to his family. His travels led him to France where he took up residence in a monastery and lived as a monk. He devoted the next twenty years of his life to the study of Christianity. Succat studied hard so he could become a priest. During that time in history, when a man went through a ceremony called an ordination to become a priest, he also received a new name. It was during his ordination when Maewyn Succat was given the name Patricius, the Latin word for Patrick. [12]

Patrick worked hard as a priest. He was very loyal to the Christian faith and was considered a respected part of the Catholic Church. In the year 432, Patrick was given a new and important position of leadership in the Church. He was made a bishop. [13]

Despite his good work and success with the Catholic Church, Patrick could not stop thinking about the days when he was held as a slave. He thought about the people he had met. Many people in Ireland believed in magic and spells. They participated in the Celtic religion and followed teachings of religious advisers called Druids. Druids did not pray to the Christian God but instead they prayed to many gods. They cast spells and held religious ceremonies in the forests. Many

Druids

Druidism is an ancient religion that may have originated in prehistoric European society.[14] The Druids were the elite members of Druidism and are believed to have acted as judges, teachers, doctors, historians, and priests. The word, *Druid*, is thought to mean "wise one."[15]

The Druids taught followers that the human spirit was a part of the natural world and that after death, it passed on to a joyous afterlife. Some modern scholars believe human sacrifices practiced by the Druids were not horrific events, but willful acts of passage to a new life.[16] The Druids claimed that the organs could give them clues to what would happen in the future.[17]

Today, Druidism is still practiced in many parts of the world. Although human sacrifice is no longer practiced, modern Druidism seeks to find a balance between nature and the human spirit.[18]

people feared the Druids. They did not want the Druids to become angry and cast evil spells on them.

Patrick believed in a God of kindness and hope. He wanted to teach the people of Ireland about his God and the religion called Christianity. He traveled back to Ireland and worked hard to teach the people about Christianity.

Followers of Druidism believed the human spirit was connected with the elements of their environment. It is said that the Druids knew how to communicate with animals, plants, stones, as well as the sea, sky, and other spirits. They did not need to learn about the new, Christian god, they did not want to hear what Patrick had to say.[19]

At first, the Irish did not want to learn from Patrick. But Patrick was a masterful teacher. He respected the old ways of the Irish and decided to use parts of the Celtic religion to help them understand Christianity. For example, the Irish once prayed to the sun as a god. Patrick added a sun symbol to the Christian cross to help the Irish feel more comfortable with the Christian symbol. Another example involved fire. Druids once welcomed the coming of spring with huge bonfires. Patrick decided to use bonfires in the Irish celebration of Easter.[20]

Druids are said to have built this circle of stone in Ireland.

One story tells of Patrick lighting a bonfire to celebrate Easter on a hill just across a valley from another hill where Druids were worshiping their own gods with fire. The Druids ordered Patrick to put his fire out. Patrick answered with a strong message stating that the fire he had started,

Christianity, is strong and can never be put out. The fire story is just one more story that shows how clever St. Patrick was in bringing the messages of the Christian faith to Ireland. Over many years of teaching, the Irish people began to accept Patrick's ideas.[21]

The Celebrations Begin

Patrick's life ended on March 17 in the year 461. After his death, the Catholic Church named him a saint, Saint Patrick. Many of his followers held annual celebrations to honor his life's work. At first the celebrations were small and unorganized. Isolated groups of St. Patrick's followers gathered to drink, feast, and dance in unofficial celebrations.

In the 1600s, the Irish celebrated many saints. The church calendar in Ireland was marked with over thirty-five days set aside for feasting in honor of various saints. But, because of Saint Patrick's unique dedication to Ireland, his day is still honored while most of the other saints have been long forgotten.[22]

In 1607, Saint Patrick's Day was listed as an official holiday on the Irish calendar. This distinction brought forth larger and more elaborate festivities honoring Saint Patrick. March 17 was not only a recognized religious holiday; it was also a joyous civic event. March 17 religious services were followed by music, dance, playful games, and feasting.

By the late 1700s, the celebrations had become quite elaborate. It was at this time when some of the traditional symbols originated. Pins and ribbons were used to decorate clothing and hats. Shamrocks were carried in bundles, worn on clothing, and sometimes eaten to help sweeten the breath.

Church bells sounded throughout cities. The bells were sometimes so loud that people complained of the deafening noise.[23] Many Irish considered the public celebrations honoring Saint Patrick as wild and excessive. Others looked forward to the annual gatherings with great excitement.

In the late eighteenth century, Saint Patrick's Day celebrations began to take on a more sophisticated flair. Dublin Castle, in Ireland's capital city, began hosting refined private parties to mark March 17. These affairs were not open to the public. Invitations were sent only to Irish society's elite members. Wealthy citizens gathered at the castle for a decadent banquet complete with an orchestra and dancing. It was not uncommon for the festivities to linger into the early morning hours

Ireland is home to many ancient castles.

when hungry guests were treated with a late-night food buffet at three o'clock in the morning.[24]

The parties at Dublin Castle provided more than just entertainment for a select few. The castle's gala event stimulated the community's

Dublin Castle

Dublin Castle, built under the direction of King John of England in 1204,[25] was used by the English as a political command center until 1922[26] when the building was given to the people of Ireland. In its day, each corner of the rectangular-shaped castle was capped with a tall, round tower.[27] Although today it is surrounded by modern construction, at one time the castle sat next to the River Poddle which brought boats to its front door.[28]

The castle was once lived in by lords and kings. It was also used as a treasury to hold England's riches, and as a prison that held many Irish patriots who wished to end the rule of England in their land.[29] Today, the same area is used to inaugurate Irish presidents.[30]

A large part of the castle was destroyed by fire in 1684.[31] The south towers and part of the connecting wall are all that remain of the original structure. Visitors now walk through a structure that was built during a massive reconstruction which started in 1730 and ended in 1800.[32]

economy. Costumes, food, decorations, and drinks needed to be prepared. Musicians and entertainers had to be hired. Many skilled workers and entertainers earned a handsome income by participating in the celebration.

More Than One Saint

Many historians believe that the stories relating to St. Patrick may have been pulled from the lives of more than one man. Some scholars say that the stories from two separate lives were used to create one cherished saint. Others believe that as many as five lives could have been pieced together to create the image of the man now known as St. Patrick.[33]

Even though some of the facts can be questioned, there are things that we can be certain of. St. Patrick, who is considered by many to be the most popular Irish icon in history, was not Irish at all. He was an Englishman, plucked from his home at an early age by Irish raiders. His adventures and life's work have had a profound influence on Ireland's history. The day set aside to honor him, St. Patrick's Day, is a festive time still recognized and celebrated today.

This painting by Albert Anker shows a girl peeling potatoes.

The Cultural Significance of St. Patrick's Day

The events that shaped Ireland's history contain both moments of joy and extreme suffering. St. Patrick's Day may be a day of celebration, but it is also a time when people remember the hard times many Irish were forced to struggle through. Between 1845 and 1851, the people of Ireland faced massive starvation. This span of time is historically referred to as Ireland's Great Famine, the Great Hunger, or the Potato Blight.[1]

Beginning in the sixteenth century, most Irish depended heavily on potatoes for survival. The country's rich soil was perfect for growing potatoes, and the Irish ate great amounts of them. A typical Irish man was known to devour several pounds of potatoes each day. Potatoes were also fed to the pigs, which in turn provided the Irish people with an important and inexpensive source of meat as well as a source of income for the farmers who raised and sold livestock.[2]

For many years the potato crop was strong and thriving, until one day a destructive parasite appeared. A fungus called *Phytophthora* was accidentally brought to Ireland in shipments of bird droppings that came from North America and Europe. The bird droppings were used by Irish farmers as fertilizer to help the potato crops grow. The poisonous fungus was eventually found in the bird droppings, but the horrible discovery was made too late. The fertilizer had already been spread over most of Ireland's potato fields.[3]

The fungus infected the potato crop with a disease called blight that destroyed the potatoes underground as they grew.[4] Blight causes plants to wither and rot. At harvest time, Irish farmers were devastated when they found their entire crops of potatoes had turned rotten.

Struggle and Starvation

For six years, the fungus destroyed Ireland's potato crops. Without potatoes, many people in Ireland had no food and, with no potatoes to sell, they had no way to earn a living. Starvation and disease caused many Irish to become unhealthy and weak. Many people died. The people who survived had no way to take care of the sick and no way to bury all of the dead.

The *Times* reported accounts of death on January 10, 1847:

> In the parish of Kilmore, fourteen died on Sunday; three of these were buried in coffins, eleven were buried without other covering than the rags they wore when alive.
>
> The Rev. Mr. Clancy visits a farm, and there, in one house, "he administered the last rites of religion to six persons." On a subsequent occasion, he "prepared for death a father and daughter lying in the same bed."[5]

The Great Hunger had transformed Ireland into a country filled with sadness, disease, and death.

Many Irish began to feel their heavy sadness mix with anger toward the British government. At that time in history, the British government controlled Ireland. When the potato famine began, the British did little to help battle the resulting starvation and disease. The Irish demanded that Britain send help, but the British responded with tyranny rather than sympathy and began evicting farmers who could not pay their rent. As more people were evicted, Irish anger grew. Some families refused to abandon their homes when they were told to leave, but their efforts were in vain. The British government sent groups of police officers to forcefully evict families. An eyewitness gives a detailed description of such a scene:

> The scene was frightful; women running, wailing with pieces of their property and clinging to door-posts from which they had to be forcibly torn; men cursing, children screaming with fright. That night the people slept in the ruins; the next day they were driven out, the foundations of the house were torn up and razed, and no neighbor was allowed to take them in.[6]

The British government claimed they did send help to the starving masses in Ireland. They lowered the rent for many workers, but with no money at all, even a small amount of rent was impossible for most families to pay. The government ordered the sale of bread flour called Indian meal. The flour was intended to be used to make an inexpensive

Why the British Controlled Ireland

During the 1100s, the English thought about invading Ireland for their own economic gain. In 1154, King Henry II gained control of England.[7] Between the years, 1169 and 1171, the Normans took over many parts of Ireland.[8] King Henry went to Ireland in 1171 with a large army. The Irish gave up, and hoped for protection from the Normans.[9]

Prince John, Henry II's youngest son, became Lord of Ireland in 1177.[10] John arrived in Ireland in 1185.[11] England developed large areas of land, while the Irish were forced to work for very low wages.[12] In 1541, Henry VIII declared himself the king of Ireland.

yet nutritious bread to help curb starvation. Many Irish were insulted by the sale of Indian meal. They felt the flour was "nothing better than sawdust" and that asking them to pay money for it was ridiculous.[13]

Many people speculated that the famine was part of a plan set into action by the British. Some Irish felt that by stimulating poverty and starvation, the British government would be able to absorb Ireland's land as part of England. Others believed the famine was a plot to commit genocide, the killing of the entire Irish population.[14]

During the 1800s, the people of Ireland endured a famine. They lost their crops and starved. People stormed businesses looking for work and money.

Beliefs like these caused widespread uprising of Irish people against the British. Hatred and anger toward the British grew stronger and stronger until some Irish began to act out violently by destroying property and murdering British landowners.

Years Without Celebration

The mid-1800s did not provide the Irish with much to celebrate. Historical records of Saint Patrick's

Day celebrations in the mid-1800s are basically nonexistent. Some historians believe that newspapers simply did not publish stories about celebrations because the times were so grim. These historians speculate that newspaper companies may have thought stories describing festive celebrations during such trying times would be upsetting to readers who were faced with extreme poverty.

Historians have, however, found evidence of some areas of Ireland where celebrations did take place. The St. Patrick's Day Ball held at Dublin Castle is one event that continued on through Ireland's black years. The ball was held only for members of Ireland's high society, which consisted of government officials who were connected to England and ruled the land from behind the walls of Dublin Castle. These government officials were heavily insulated by wealth and did not feel the impact of Ireland's dark days. Watching the rich celebrate during such difficult times caused anger to grow more intense in the hearts of those Irish who were suffering.[15]

St. Patrick's Day provided a time for angry groups of Irish to gather in protest. Because of the holiday's religious significance, many employers suspended work in honor of the day. Irish activists used their time away from work to voice their displeasure in the government. One example of an Irish activist group was the Tenant Right Movement. The Tenant Right Movement was a group of Irishmen who fought against the high rents and evictions subjected upon them by the British. On St. Patrick's Day 1850, the group encouraged over forty thousand people to gather in protest against the British.[16]

Mass Exodus

Many Irish did more than protest. They left the country. Beginning in the 1840s, millions of Irish piled onto crowded ships and rode across the sea to new lands in search of a better life. Many emigrants set their sights on the United States while others dreamed of starting over in Canada or Australia.[17] Though the Irish who stepped onto the ships dreamed of a better life, their future would not be as bright as they hoped.

Irish emigrants found themselves squeezed onto overcrowded ships with unsanitary conditions very similar to those found on the African slave ships that had sailed a century before. Great numbers of passengers carrying diseases boarded the ships, spreading sickness and death to many people. Some estimates say that nearly

40 percent of the emigrants died either on the ships or soon after they disembarked.[18] Because of the huge mortality rate, the ships were given the grim nickname of "coffin ships."

Stephen de Vere, a passenger on such a ship, wrote about his trip in 1847:

> Hundreds of poor people, men, women, and children of all ages huddled together without light, without air, wallowing in filth and breathing a fetid atmosphere. . . . The supply of water, hardly enough for cooking and drinking, does not allow for washing.[19]

During the time of the Irish famine, an estimated 1.3 million people left Ireland to set up homes in new lands. As many as 70 percent of those people immigrated to the United States, 28 percent went to Canada, and 2 percent to Australia.[20]

Difficult Times in a New Land

The Irish who walked off the coffin ships were sick, weak, uneducated, and poor. As they stepped onto American soil they were not greeted by cheerful welcoming committees. Many times the ships were boarded by greedy men who swiftly took the newly arrived Irish to tenement houses. There, they were charged inflated fees to rent run-down, dirty living spaces. Many Irish immigrants were forced to live on the streets where they begged and scavenged for food. To their disappointment, many Irish found the poverty and hardship in the United States to be no different from what they had left behind in Ireland.[21] Feelings of homesickness and a longing for the life they once knew became heavy in the hearts of many immigrants. Some Irish expressed their sadness through songs such as this one:

> Oh fare thee well Ireland, my own dear native land,
>
> It breaks my heart to see friends part for it's then that the tear drops fall.
>
> I'm on my way to Amerikay, will I ere see my home once more,
>
> For now I leave my own true love on Paddy's Green Shamrock Shore.[22]

Most immigrants who settled in the United States stayed in the eastern cities where their ships pulled into port. Boston and New York were both flooded with huge influxes of Irish immigrants. By 1847, there were thirty-seven thousand Irish immigrants in Boston, which made up over one third of the city's total population.[23] Philadelphia, Chicago, Charleston, and New Orleans are other

Many Irish people sailed to the United States in hopes of a better life.

cities that absorbed many of the newly arrived Irish population.[24]

Because of their lack of education and weakened physical state, the booming influx of Irish men had a difficult time finding good work. They were forced to take on menial jobs doing tasks such as sweeping sidewalks, tending horses, cleaning stables, and cutting fish. This type of unskilled labor did little to provide food and shelter for a family, so the Irish women took it upon themselves to search for work. The jobs available to women brought in more money than the jobs many men had. By working in hotels as part of cleaning staffs or in homes as domestic servants, some women were able to earn enough money to support their families.[25]

Although times were hard, Irish immigrants did not waste time dwelling on their difficult conditions. They formed tightly bonded Irish communities within the cities that they settled. They worked hard to teach their children skills that would bring better times. Over the next several decades, their hard work began to pay off. New generations of Irish were able to find work as plumbers, carpenters, policemen, and firefighters.[26]

Irish Pride

Part of the Irish success can be placed on the importance of St. Patrick's Day. The holiday provided the Irish, no matter what city or what country they lived, a day to celebrate their heritage. By rallying together, marching in parades and sharing their heritage with others, the Irish were able to reflect on their accomplishments and instill a sense of pride in both themselves and future generations. The celebrations brought a positive light to the Irish community during a time when many Americans looked at the immigrants with disdain.

St. Patrick's Day parades played an important role in spurring political awareness. Irish politicians used the parades as a vehicle to spread their beliefs to the masses. On St. Patrick's Day, 1766, a group of soldiers paraded through the streets of New York City. In 1841, more than two thousand marchers took to the streets in Boston, Massachusetts, during the city's first St. Patrick's Day parade. By 1849, the New York parade had become an annual occurance on the city's calendar of official civic events.[27]

Irish political activists worked hard to cast a positive light on their culture. They began to enjoy the results of their labor as more and more Irish moved into important leadership roles. In 1828, Andrew Jackson, the son of Irish immigrants, was elected president of the United States. One hundred years later, the state of New York elected Al Smith, an Irish Catholic, as governor. One of the most well-known U.S. presidents in history, John F. Kennedy, was also an Irish Catholic.[28]

The list of Irish success is quite long and spans the entire spectrum of American culture. Henry Ford, the founder of the Ford automotive company, was the son of immigrants from Cork, Ireland. The honored educator, Kate Kennedy, who emigrated from County Meath, Ireland, and worked as a schoolteacher in San Francisco, opened the door for many other Irish women who wanted to work as teachers. Animator Walt Disney, singer Bing Crosby, artist Georgia O'Keeffe, and Supreme Court justice Sandra Day O'Connor are all well-known Irish Americans who made a huge impact on American culture.[29]

Throughout history, the people of Ireland have been faced with extreme obstacles of hardship. Their strength, pride, and ability to pull one

Kate Kennedy

Kate Kennedy was an Irish woman who survived the potato famine of the 1840s. She believed that hard work was its own reward, and that working hard was one's way of contributing to society.[30]

Kennedy's family came to New York in the 1800s. She worked at an embroidery factory while studying to be a teacher. Her family moved west, and in 1857, Kennedy was hired to teach in San Francisco, California. She became a principal in 1859. She received a much lower salary than the men who were also principals. Kennedy fought for the equal treatment of women in the workplace. Today, her name represents strength, equality for women, and excellence in education.[31]

Singer Bing Crosby and artist Georgia O'Keeffe are Irish Americans whose careers had a big impact on the American people.

another through such times have helped them become a respected and successful cultural group that is openly welcomed in many countries all over the world. Each year, on one very special day, non-Irish cultures join the Irish as they celebrate their accomplishments of today. For the Irish, St. Patrick's Day is both a day to remember the past and a time to look forward to the future.

A large dragon floats his way through the streets of Dublin, Ireland, during a St. Patrick's Day parade.

Who Celebrates St. Patrick's Day?

St. Patrick's Day is celebrated by Irish and non-Irish, Catholics and non-Catholics, adults and children. Families often celebrate together at home while groups of young friends gather at parties. It is common for politicians to march in parades while thousands of people from many different backgrounds stand along the sidewalk to watch. The green holiday, St. Patrick's Day, is a holiday that seems to have no boundaries. People on every continent have joined in the fun of the celebration and adopted many Irish customs as their own. From Ireland to Canada to Australia, it seems that on March 17, everyone is Irish.

Religious Celebration

Hundreds of years ago, when the holiday first began, St. Patrick's Day was considered a solemn day set aside to remember the life of St. Patrick. The holiday was considered first as a day of worship but also allowed for feasting and relaxation.[1] Today, many Irish Catholics and Protestants begin St. Patrick's Day at church. During St. Patrick's Day mass, they sing, pray, and listen to their priests speak about the life of St. Patrick.

Each year, March 17 falls during a time of year known on the Christian calendar as Lent. During Lent, Christians remember the life and death of Jesus. During the Lenten season, it is a traditional custom for Christians to fast, or give up certain luxury foods such as meat or sweet treats.[2] But, because St. Patrick's Day is recognized by the Church as a day of feasting, the rules of Lent are changed for one day. On St. Patrick's Day, the rules of fasting are lifted and people are allowed to indulge in eating, celebrating, and dancing.[3]

The Children Prepare

In the early eighteenth century, the focus of St. Patrick's Day was purely religious. Children spent the weeks before the holiday preparing for the day's arrival. They made crosses to wear to church and memorized special holiday hymns to sing.

The crosses made by boys and girls were different from each other. Boys used small squares of white paper and painted them with many colors. The paints once used may seem unusual to modern children. Boys used egg yolk to paint their crosses yellow and chewed young grass to make them green. Once finished with his cross, each boy attached the decoration to his cap and wore it proudly to church. Girls crafted more complicated crosses. Using cardboard, colorful ribbons, and flowers, each girl created a fancy ornament. The cross was finished with a tiny green rosette that was glued to the center. Each girl displayed her cross by pinning it to the top of her dress.[4]

On the morning of St. Patrick's Day, the children awoke with excitement. They knew that for one day the rules of Lent would be ignored. They would be allowed to indulge in sweets and fun. Attending a church service, or mass, was the first event of the day. At church the children sang the traditional hymn, "Hail Glorious St. Patrick."

When mass was over many children participated in a shamrock hunt that was often held on the church grounds. Writer Mary Moylan tells about her childhood experiences with shamrock hunting:

> And the hunt for the shamrock in those days! It was easy to spot in the fields where we knew it grew. We would pull it up by the roots to keep it fresh in a glass for the morning and then we would pin it to our coats and wear it all day.[5]

Feasting With Friends

After a day of worship, the children often followed their mother home, where they worked together to prepare a hearty feast. Meat was almost always served as the main dish as the family knew the rules of Lent would not allow it on the following day. Savory dishes such as lamb stew and roasted chicken filled the air with warm, comforting smells. Children also helped prepare other comforting foods such as potatoes, cabbage, and soda bread.[6]

After filling their stomachs with a fine meal, many traditional Irish families joined together with groups of other families for music, dancing, and storytelling. These sorts of gatherings, called ceilis [KAY-lees], often continued until the late hours of the night.[7]

In schools today, students learn about St. Patrick's Day. These girls eat green food their teacher brought in to honor St. Patrick's Day.

Although some modern Irish families still hold ceilis, non-Irish families may be more familiar with common traditions. Today's children sometimes enjoy licking the green icing off of cupcakes while they wait for their turn to search for chocolate coins. Some children celebrate St. Patrick's Day by making leprechaun hats and shamrocks from green paper, while other children read Irish poetry and listen to storytellers who share traditional Irish tales.

Political Parades

Watching a parade is a St. Patrick's Day tradition enjoyed by both adults and children. Unlike some of the popular parades of today, early St. Patrick's Day parades did not include marching bands or dance troupes. In the mid-nineteenth century, the Irish began using the traditional St. Patrick's Day parade as a political tool. At that time, many of the parade participants were campaigning politicians. Politicians realized that the annual parades provided them with the opportunity to meet hundreds, if not thousands, of potential voters. In 1948, Harry S. Truman became the first United States president to lead a St. Patrick's Day parade through the streets of New York City.[8]

Holiday Proclamation

In 1995, the United States Congress proclaimed March as Irish-American Heritage Month. Since that year, the serving U.S. president continues to bring attention to the month by delivering an

Why Were St. Patrick's Day Parades So Political?

Parades often attract politicians who wish to make contact with potential voters. St. Patrick's Day parades have a strong tradition of serving as a platform for political issues. In the mid-1800s, when the Irish immigration into the United States was at its peak, the Irish had serious issues.

Many people in the United States did not like the idea of the new immigrants coming into their cities. In 1844, in Philadelphia, mobs burned Irish homes and attacked Catholic churches. Irish immigrants found themselves denied voting rights, and were forbidden to hold public office in some states.[9]

The Irish responded by joining forces. In 1848, two parades combined to create one, large parade. This gesture showed the country that the Irish were an important population.[10]

annual proclamation. On March 5, 2004, President Bush stated in his proclamation:

> Millions of Americans trace their ancestry to Ireland's shores. During Irish-American Heritage Month, we recognize these proud citizens and their important contributions to America.

In Boston, Massachusetts, the members of the Boston Gaelic Fire Brigade march down the street on St. Patrick's Day.

Irish Americans have helped settle the American frontier, build our cities, and defend our homeland. Through their service in government and the military, they have helped to uphold our democracy and advance liberty and peace around the world.[11]

While the United States does not recognize St. Patrick's Day as a legal holiday, the city of Boston does. In Boston, March 17 is Evacuation Day, a holiday that commemorates the day the British left Boston Harbor during the Revolutionary War. It is said that George Washington used the password "St. Patrick" to confirm the British evacuation on March 17, 1776. In Boston, March 17 is a day to remember two great leaders, St. Patrick and George Washington, as well as celebrate the British defeat.[12]

All over the world, regardless of their political position or heritage, people join together to celebrate St. Patrick's Day. Canada and Australia are two countries that enjoy showing off their Irish pride. In 1909, Canadians built a monument in Gross Isle, Quebec, honoring the Irish emigrants who died while trying to reach Canada.[13] Australians once illustrated their Irish pride by building the world's largest shamrock. Standing thirty feet high, the artificial leaf was the highlight

The Montreal St. Patrick's Day parade in Canada is said to be the oldest in North America.

of Australia's 1992 St. Patrick's Day celebration. During the same year, Australians planted fifty thousand trees across the country to honor their Irish heritage.[14] Another Irish-Australian custom has no connection to Ireland at all. Potato lobbing is a game similar to horseshoes. Players stand at opposite ends of a playing field and test their aim by tossing potatoes into a wooden crate. The game has become so customary that most Australians think the tradition came straight from Ireland. However the game began, it has become an Australian favorite. Even though many of their St. Patrick's Day traditions did not originate in Ireland, Canada and Australia are two countries that demonstrate their Irish pride on a grand scale.[15]

People all over the world, young, old, Irish and non-Irish, enjoy celebrating St. Patrick's Day. The holiday is a time for people to celebrate and remember not only St. Patrick himself, but the strength of the Irish culture.

Symbols of St. Patrick's Day

In early March, bulletin boards and hallways in schools across the United States are cleared of their winter themes. As spring draws near, paper snowflakes, leafless trees, and cotton ball snowmen are replaced with shamrocks, leprechauns, and pots of gold. These symbols signal the coming of a special holiday, St. Patrick's Day.

St. Patrick's Day is a holiday filled with symbolic traditions. Feasts of Irish stew, soda bread, corned beef, and cabbage are accompanied by festive music and dancing. Banners decorated

Legends say St. Patrick rid Ireland of all snakes.

with snakes and crosses are carried through parades. Some pubs even serve green beer. The symbols of St. Patrick's Day are easy to recognize, and, when they are seen, there is no doubt that the green holiday is on the way.

Most St. Patrick's Day symbols are connected to either legends or cultural traditions. The symbol of the snake is deeply rooted in Irish history. Legends say that St. Patrick stood on top of a great hill, raised his wooden staff into the air, and in one instant, cleared all the snakes from Ireland. The story is actually a symbolic comparison that explains St. Patrick's work in clearing Ireland of its pagan beliefs and introducing the Christian religion.[1]

The Shamrock

The connection of the shamrock to St. Patrick's Day was also made by St. Patrick. The shamrock, or clover, was part of Irish culture even before St. Patrick became part of Ireland's history. Shamrocks, or as the Celts would say, "seamrog," meaning "little clover,"[2] have been growing on Irish hillsides for thousands of years. The Celts

The shamrock is a big part of St. Patrick's Day decorations.

considered several different plants, including hop clover, white clover, and black medic, to be sacred as these plants promised the arrival of spring.

The Celts regarded the shamrock as a powerful charm used to defend the wearer against the power of witches. Irish who traveled along over swamps and through forests carried shamrocks to help ward off threats from the banshees and wicked fairies who lived there.[3]

The connection of the shamrock to St. Patrick's Day was made when St. Patrick used it as the focus of an object lesson to explain the concept of Trinity. Just as the three leaves of a shamrock make up one plant, God is made up of three parts: the Father, the Son, and the Holy Spirit.[4] The lesson was very effective in teaching the Celts about Christianity. Even today, Irish Christians recognize the shamrock as a symbol of the Trinity.

The importance of the shamrock grew even greater in the 1500s. During that century, England took control of Ireland.[5] The English rulers controlled every aspect of Irish life, including the way the Irish worshiped God and the language they spoke. In protest, the Irish pinned shamrocks to their clothing as a statement of pride and loyalty to their own culture. This practice was known as the "wearing of the green." The poem titled, "The Wearing of the Green," by Dion Boucicault, captures Irish feelings of strength and hardship. A part of the poem is written here:

> O Paddy dear, and did you hear the news that's going round?

The shamrock is forbid by law to grow on Irish
ground;

St. Patrick's Day no more we'll keep, his
colours can't be seen,

For there's a bloody law against the wearing of
the green.

I met with Napper Tandy and he took me by
the hand,

And he said, "How's poor old Ireland, and how
does she stand?"

She's the most distressful counterie that ever
yet was seen,

And they're hanging men and women for the
wearing of the green.[6]

Leprechauns

Not all that is green carries with it such memories
of sorrow. Tiny elves called leprechauns have
become a whimsical part of St. Patrick's Day
traditions. Walt Disney has been credited with
connecting the leprechaun to St. Patrick's Day. In
1959, Disney created a film called *Darby O'Gill and
the Little People*. The film portrayed leprechauns as
sprightly characters, dressed in green from head to
toe. After the release of the film, the image of the
leprechaun quickly became a well-known symbol
of St. Patrick's Day and everything Irish.[7]

Before being transformed by Disney, leprechauns were thought of as sneaky, ornery creatures. Many traditional descriptions of leprechauns tell of short men, about three feet tall, who wore a suit of red, a leather apron, and fancy shoes. Many people credit Disney with changing the leprechaun's clothes to green. Stories claim leprechauns prefer to live in forests, farmhouses, or wine cellars, where they often trade good-luck charms for supplies with humans.[8]

Most stories agree that leprechauns are master shoemakers. Irish folklore is filled with stories of fairies who love to dance. The fairies danced and danced until their shoes were completely worn with holes. Leprechauns worked at night, mending the fairies' shoes. In return for fixing their shoes, the fairies left gold coins for the leprechauns. Stories go on to say that leprechauns saved their coins in large pots. It has been said that any leprechaun captured by a human must give his

Leprechauns guard their pots of gold at the end of the rainbow.

gold away. But the instant a leprechaun's captor looks away, the tricky little sprite always seems to mysteriously disappear.[9] Today schoolchildren across the world enjoy searching for leprechauns and their treasure, which is said to be kept at the end of the rainbow.

> Do you not catch the tiny clamour,
> Busy click of an elfin hammer,
> Voice of the Lepracaun singing shrill,
> As he merrily plies his trade?
>
> William Allingham as in
> *Irish Fairy and Folk Tales* (1893),
> edited by W. B. Yeats[10]

Music

Fairies and elves are not the only creatures that enjoy music and dance. Musical celebrations have been a part of Irish culture for centuries. Besides being an enjoyable activity, music and storytelling played an important role in preserving Irish history.

The Celts did not record their traditions and history through writing. Instead they used music and songs to pass down the important events of their time. Songs were sung to tell about events in history, religion, and favorite legends. As these songs were passed through the generations, so was the ancient history of Ireland.

Queen Elizabeth I recognized the power of music in the Irish culture and put an end to all singing and music making. Because of the ability music had to bond the Irish people together, Queen Elizabeth called for all musicians to be arrested. Her efforts to silence the spirit of the Irish were unsuccessful. Even today, Irish bands play jubilant music throughout the year, but their spirit is especially strong on St. Patrick's Day.[11]

There are a few musical instruments that are unique to the Irish. A special type of bagpipe, called the uilleann [EYE-lin] pipes, is sounded by pumping air through a bag that is placed under the player's arm. Unlike the bagpipe, no part of the instrument is placed in the player's mouth. The bodhran [BO-ron] is a unique drum that is held in the player's hand. The frame, made from wood, is round. A sheet of goatskin is stretched around the frame to create the drum's head. To play the drum, a person can either hit it with his or her hand or use a special stick to tap out a rhythm. These two instruments are considered the only ones that are derived directly from the Irish culture. All other instruments, such as the fiddle, the harp, and the tin whistle, which are often thought of as Irish, have been imported into the culture from other countries. No matter where

The bodhran is an Irish drum made with goat skin stretched across the top.

the instruments come from, there is no doubt that the spirit of Ireland lives through its music.[12]

Dance

With music comes dance, another symbol of Irish culture. Traveling shows like *Riverdance* and *Lord of the Dance* have helped the flamboyant steps of Irish dance gain worldwide popularity. Dancers from these troupes have inspired young children to pour into Irish dance studios. Irish dance competitions have become seriously judged events that are attended by people from all over the world.[13]

In Irish dance, dancers focus on footwork while their arms are held stiff at their sides. In many dances, the dancers stay in one place and do not move around the stage. A unique feature of Irish dance is the tapping sounds created by the shoes of the dancers. Long ago, dancers performed on tables, barrel tops, or even on doors that had been taken down off their hinges.[14] In Irish dance, large groups of dancers often dance together in long lines or in circles. Many times a solo dancer is showcased in front of the group formations. Highly skilled dancers compete with one another for the opportunity to serve as the solo dancer. Solo dancers are the most esteemed members of an Irish dance troupe. Michael Flatley and Jean Butler are examples of two solo dancers who have achieved worldwide fame and success.[15]

Traditional Irish dance is rooted deep in the history of Ireland. It is believed that around A.D. 400, the Celts and Druids used dance in religious ceremonies to honor the elements of nature.[16] The Anglo-Norman invasion of 1161 brought with it a new type of dance. As the Anglo-Normans conquered Irish cities, a dance was performed by the invaders in the town's center. These dances involved a leader who stood in the center of a ring of dancers. The leader would sing while the dancers would echo his song with dance.[17]

In the sixteenth century, Queen Elizabeth I ordered a stop to all Irish dance in Ireland. She feared the tradition would help bond the Irish people to one another and possibly result in an uprising against English rule. However, the queen herself was quite fond of the lively steps and, in spite of her ruling, often gathered troupes together in her court to dance for her entertainment.[18]

Irish dance is very popular today. Many people compete and put on shows.

In the 1700s, the ban against dancing was not strictly enforced. The Irish began welcoming royalty into their country with dance. As ships arrived, groups of dancers performed traditional dances as a way of greeting their important visitors. Oftentimes the dances began at a slow pace, then grew faster as the dancing continued.[19]

Later that century, dance masters began to appear in villages throughout Ireland. Dance masters were highly skilled dancers who traveled from village to village, teaching the steps and traditions of Irish dance. It is said that many of the dance masters' students did not know the difference between their right and left foot. To help their students learn, dance masters would tie a bit of straw or hay to the dancers' feet. The dance masters would then instruct their students to either lift their "hay" foot or kick with their "straw" foot.[20]

Dance masters grew attached to their students and were very possessive of their territories. One dance master did not dare to enter another's village. Often, dance masters would meet at fairs and challenge each other to public dance competitions. Stories say that the contests ended only when one of the dancers collapsed from exhaustion.[21]

Food

On St. Patrick's Day, exhausted dancers need not look far to find food to replenish their energy. Savory scents of corned beef, cabbage, Irish stew with lamb, and soda bread drift from kitchens across America and the world on March 17. Although food has long been part of St. Patrick's Day celebrations, the traditional main course has changed over time. What most people may think of as the most traditional Irish meat was never really consumed in Ireland. Corned beef did not become part of the St. Patrick's Day celebration until more recent times. Stories say that Irish immigrants living in New York City's lower east side learned of corned beef, the less expensive alternative to Irish bacon, from their Jewish friends.[22]

Corned beef may be a relatively recent change to Irish tradition, but serving meat as a main course on St. Patrick's Day has been a custom for hundreds of years. In fact, the tradition comes straight from St. Patrick himself. The story explains that, during his religious training, St. Patrick was tempted to eat meat, which he had been forbidden to do. His desire led him to hide some pork with the intention of eating it later. After giving in to his weakness, Patrick was consumed with guilt. He prayed to God for forgiveness and promised never to eat meat again for the rest of his life. After his prayers, an angel came to St. Patrick and asked him to throw the hidden meat into the water. St. Patrick did as he was told. The legend states that the moment he cast the meat into the water, it turned to fish. From that day forward, the Irish have been known to drop their meat into water and announce that they would be eating "fishes of St. Patrick." The Irish honor St. Patrick and celebrate Lent by eating meat on March 17, just as they have since the early 1100s.[23]

There are other symbolic foods that are often found on tables during traditional St. Patrick's Day

Many people have corned beef and cabbage on St. Patrick's Day.

celebration meals. The potato reminds Irish of the difficult times during the potato blight that their countrymen once had to survive. At the end of the hearty meal, one last toast called, the "drowning of the shamrock" is often made. In this custom, a leaf which had been worn on someone's cap or coat throughout the day is placed at the bottom of a drinking cup. Toasts are then made in honor of each guest. At the end of the praises and blessings, the shamrock is removed from the bottom of the cup, then tossed over one's left shoulder.[24]

An Irish Blessing:

May your heart be warm and happy
With the lilt of Irish laughter
Every day in every way
And forever and ever after.

The symbols associated with St. Patrick's Day are used to remind people of the challenges and events that have shaped the Irish culture. Leprechauns, shamrocks, music, dance, and food are familiar symbols that signal the coming of spring and the celebration of all that is Irish.

Marchers parade down
a street in Moscow for
St. Patrick's Day.

How St. Patrick's Day Is Celebrated Today

Over a span of hundreds of years, St. Patrick's Day has grown from a simple day of relaxation recognized by a few of the saint's closest followers to an international holiday, celebrated by people all over the world. Today, countries far from Ireland participate in the customs of March 17. In 1985, the West Indian country, Montserrat, declared St. Patrick's Day a national holiday, while in 1992, Moscow, Russia, held its first annual

St. Patrick's Day parade. The year 2003 brought more than one hundred dancers and musicians to France where they gathered at the huge Paris stadium, Stade de France. During the celebration in France, over twenty thousand fans danced on the stadium's playing field to the music of some of today's most popular Irish artists. With its abundance of worldwide attention, St. Patrick's Day has become a holiday that is recognized in almost every country on earth.[1]

Celebrations in Ireland

One might think that Ireland, the country in which the holiday began, would hold the most elaborate St. Patrick's Day celebrations of all. Many Irish citizens consider St. Patrick's Day to be a fine day of relaxation but definitely not an over-the-top extravaganza. In Ireland, the day is traditionally a religious celebration and, for hundreds of years, the Irish did next to nothing to honor the holiday. Some images of celebrations held decades ago were actually quite negative. A reporter from the *Irish Voice* describes his dismal St. Patrick's Day memories:

> Dublin was most definitely not the place to be on St. Patrick's Day. It was usually a rain-soaked, mournful day, punctuated with

soggy shamrocks and a parade as faded as the 1950 . . . we stood there bored to distraction.[2]

Luckily, that negative tone has passed. In recent years, Ireland has made many successful attempts to raise the country's enthusiasm toward St. Patrick's Day. Groups of innovative Irish businessmen saw the holiday as an opportunity to attract tourist spending. In the mid-1900s, the idea of holding St. Patrick's Day parades similar to the extravagant events held in the United States began to gain popularity. Parade planners went so far as to bring American marching bands and cheerleaders overseas to march in Dublin's St. Patrick's Day parade.[3] At first, the idea of large, flashy parades sparked excitement, but by 1970, most Irish recognized the parade as nothing more than a scheme to bring American money into the country. Because they were more accustomed to a traditional, religious holiday, many Irish lost enthusiasm for the flashy celebrations. Despite the drain of Irish support, the huge influx of American money generated by the parades caused the celebration to grow larger each year. As time passed, the parades held in Ireland became almost purely American. Irish author Joseph O'Connor wrote, "I was sure the first Americans I saw in the flesh were at the St. Patrick's Day parade in Dublin."[4]

In 2005, these women wear elaborate costumes during a St. Patrick's Day parade in Dublin, Ireland.

By 1990 the Dublin parade consisted of six thousand participants. Over one thousand of those were from the United States and other countries.[5]

In 1995, the sour Irish attitude toward the St. Patrick's Day celebrations in Ireland began to change. That year, the Irish government began a national campaign to create a world-class St. Patrick's Day celebration. In the year 2000, officials lengthened the day-long St. Patrick's Day celebration to encompass a five-day St. Patrick's Festival. Now with over thirty parades held in the Republic of Ireland, the St. Patrick's Festival has become a destination for tourists from around the world.[6]

Centered in Dublin, Ireland, the St. Patrick's Festival offers a wide range of entertainment, food, and activities. In 2004, the Festival Music Village offered festival goers a selection of over twenty different musical acts over the course of the festival week. With bands playing traditional Irish music, techno, jazz, rock, folk, and contemporary music, even the most particular music fans were able to hear something they enjoyed.[7]

Irish citizens who wished to discuss their visions for Ireland's future gathered for the 2004 St. Patrick's Day Symposium. Here, groups of Irish scholars explored their views on Irish values, the economy, and ideas concerning social and cultural progress. Delegates from the symposium went away feeling quite positive about the experience and expressed their feelings about the day with comments such as "It forced dialogue and debate and was very thought provoking" and "It was a wonderful gathering—there was a great sense of community."[8]

In 2004, a community hub of Dublin, Merrion Square, was the center for many different types of entertainment. Roaming performance artists, games, and carnival rides attracted both Irish families and tourists. Something rather unusual, a giant inflatable bubble filled with tunnels and mysterious lighting, was a highlight of the square. Created by Alan Parkinson, the luminarium is an air-filled maze illuminated by colored lights. The luminarium was set up for the St. Patrick's Day Festival, and visitors both young and old were entranced by its beauty.[9]

While sounds of carnival rides and games fill the air near Merrion Square, echoes of stomping feet and clapping hands resound from Earlsfort Terrace. The Terrace is home to Dublin's annual ceili. The ceili offers people a place to gather together where they can enjoy music, song, and dancing. The Dublin ceili features traditional

Irish dance forms such as round and line dances. In 2004, an estimated fifteen thousand people attended the ceili where they enjoyed dancing for more than four hours.[10]

A wide variety of other events are held annually throughout Dublin during the St. Patrick's Festival. Irish Visions is a showcase of top-notch Irish art, design, and craft. Museums, galleries and public spaces are filled with paintings, sculptures, photographs, and performance artists from different parts of Ireland. The Roar of the City is an event that highlights the motor industry. Each night, a different motor vehicle group parades through town. Some of the groups include the Dublin Cycling Campaign, the Land Rover Club of Ireland, and the Dublin Cruisers. The 2004 festival parade contained over thirty-five thousand participants. Marching bands, Italian flag-wavers, and a grand finale visit from a live lion entertained spectators who lined the streets.[11]

Those who wish to learn more about their community can participate in a citywide treasure hunt. The treasure hunt challenged participants to answer questions about Ireland's capital city, Dublin. Questions such as "Do you know how high the Smithfield Chimney is?" or "Can you guess who is buried in St. Patrick's Cathedral?"

**Fireworks fill the Dublin sky at the end of the
St. Patrick's Day celebration.**

were sure to challenge as well as teach a bit of Irish
culture to all those who participated.[12]

Festival planners make a point to end the St.
Patrick's Day Festival with a bang. A nighttime
special effects show is a favorite event for both Irish
and foreign visitors. Described as a "pyromusical,"

the show incorporates fire and dance in a fantastic visual display. Ten distinct sections of over four thousand firework firings and special effects are choreographed to music with split-second accuracy. A giant radio system called the Towers of Power is set up by a local radio station to fill the night with breathtaking sound. The show is a sight that is not soon forgotten by those who are lucky enough to experience its glory.[13] With its wide variety of activities and functions, the St. Patrick's Day Festival has brought a celebration to Ireland that the Irish can be proud to share with the rest of the world.

Celebrations in the United States

Unlike Ireland, where the St. Patrick's Day celebrations are primarily religious, the more secular celebrations held in the United States have no trouble connecting the holiday with fanfare and excitement. With over 37.8 million American citizens of Irish descent, enthusiasm toward St. Patrick's Day in the United States is not surprising.[14] Over one hundred American cities hold St. Patrick's Day parades.[15] Parties, contests, dances, and feasts are just a sampling of the activities that take place in almost every major American city on St. Patrick's Day.

This band from New Jersey marches down Fifth Avenue in New York City's St. Patrick's Day parade.

The first St. Patrick's Day parade took place in New York City, March 17, 1762. Most accounts say that the first parade was a spontaneous gathering of servicemen who met with each other on their way to a St. Patrick's Day breakfast. The band members who accompanied them began to play and the remaining men decided to display their military banners while marching behind. The group attracted a mass of spectators, and from that day, the tradition of the St. Patrick's Day parade has become quite an event.[16]

Today the New York parade includes over 150,000 participants who march over one mile before stopping at St. Patrick's Cathedral. There, the highest Catholic Church official, the cardinal of New York, performs a blessing on the entire crowd. An estimated 3 million people stand along New York's Fifth Avenue to watch the four-hour St. Patrick's Day parade.[17]

New York is home to other festive traditions. People wearing green clothes, funny green hats, and carrying green flowers are not uncommon sights along the parade route. Throughout the day, one might be lucky enough to spot a café serving green bagels or take a sip of green water spurting from a fountain. Chinese restaurants have been known to serve green noodles and rice while those with a taste for Italian food can often find green lasagna on the menu.[18] At night, New York's skyline is highlighted by a spectacular scene: a green Empire State Building.[19]

American Irish spirit runs from the East Coast all the way to the Pacific Northwest. Seattle, Washington, hosts its own tribute to St. Patrick. In 2005, the city sponsored its eighth annual Irish Reels Film Festival in which films produced by independent Irish filmmakers were showcased. Another annual Seattle event is the Irish Soda Bread Contest, where contestants compete against one another to find out who prepared the tastiest bread. The city also holds a mini-parade to mark the route for the main parade. The main parade begins with an Irish flag-raising ceremony. One of the most attended events of the celebration is the St. Patrick's Day Dash. The dash is a four-mile, downhill footrace that is normally attended by over fifteen thousand participants. Seattle is one more American city that is proud to celebrate St. Patrick's Day.[20]

America's heartland also hosts a wide variety of St. Patrick's Day celebrations. The only parade that travels from one state to another begins in Rock Island, Illinois. The parade crosses the Mississippi River and ends in Davenport, Iowa.[21]

St. Patrick's Cathedral in New York City.

Trying to find New Dublin, Wisconsin, on a map is virtually impossible. Thanks to some feisty leprechauns, the town exists only for one day. Each year, a group of men from the town dress in green and head down the highway with screwdrivers in hand. As quick as a leprechaun's pot of gold can disappear, the highway sign for the town New London changes to read, New Dublin. The town's change in name brings a dash of Irish spirit to its citizens. For one day, the people of New Dublin celebrate as if they were living in the heart of Ireland.[22]

In other parts of the United States, towns with names such as St. Patrick, Missouri; Ireland, West Virginia; and Shamrock, Texas; each celebrate St. Patrick's Day with their own unique flair. Festival organizers in Ireland, West Virginia, plan a workshop to teach people how to play the harp. The town also features the only known American "road bowling" contest, where contestants bowl on the street.

St. Patrick's Day devotees who prefer to add a Texas twist to the holiday may want to spend the holiday with the townsfolk of Shamrock, Texas. Those who travel to Shamrock should expect to be greeted by a band of bearded men. The annual beard contest prompts men who wish to compete to stop shaving for months before the holiday.[23]

A Festive River

One of the most notable traditions in the world happens in the city of Chicago. Since St. Patrick's Day 1962, the city has been known for its mysterious green river. The story behind the unusual tradition began early in December 1961, when a plumber walked into the office of Steve Bailey, business manager of Chicago's Journeyman Plumbers Local Union #130. The plumber was wearing overalls marked by mysterious green stains.

The plumber explained that he had been searching waste lines for illegal dumping by pouring green dye into the sewer system. He watched the river for signs of the dye to pinpoint the source where illegal wastes were being poured into the river.

The plumber's story set Bailey's imagination in motion. He dreamed of dying the entire river green in honor of St. Patrick's Day. With an idea planted in his head by a plumber's dirty overalls, Bailey set out to figure out how to carry out his plan. After discussing the idea with town officials, he purchased a special military-grade dye that kept the river green for a whole week.

The men in this boat are dyeing the Chicago River green in honor of St. Patrick's Day.

Today, an environmentally safe dye is used in amounts that keep the river festively green for about four to five hours.[24]

When the Chicago River flows green, the pipes and drums begin to rumble. Each year, thousands of observers line the streets of Chicago to watch the annual Saint Patrick's Day parade. Since 1956, the parade has been led by the Shannon Rovers Pipe Band.

In March 2004, for the first time in history, one of the band's most cherished members, Barbara O'Hara, was not among the black-and-green kilted pipe players marching down Chicago's downtown streets. Parade organizers believe that before her recent death, O'Hara was the only person to march in every one of Chicago's St. Patrick's Day parades since the first parade held in 1956.[25]

"She was here for every single parade I can remember," said Bill McTighe of the Shannon Rovers. "I keep turning my head and looking for Barb, but she isn't there."[26]

"She was always the first one there and the last to leave, and always smiling," said John Murphy, another fellow piper.[27]

Barbara O'Hara was not the only one who looked forward to the annual Chicago parade. Each year, more than 150,000 people turn out for the parade, but only one of them can carry the title of St. Patrick's Day Queen. Each year, hundreds of young women between the ages of seventeen and twenty-six submit photos to be considered for the queen contest. The photos are evaluated by former queens who then break the list down to 180 finalists. The finalists compete at the Chicago Hilton where they are judged, and, finally, a queen is chosen to lead the city through its wide assortment of St. Patrick's Day festivities.[28]

Even the queen would have a hard time keeping up with the all the events available to those who wish to celebrate. From taking a class in Irish dance at a cultural center to pulling up a chair in a pub to listen to a traditional Irish band, the only widely celebrated day in March, St. Patrick's Day, is sure to provide a day of fun for anyone who is willing to participate.

On March 17, it seems the whole world turns green. From Ireland to the United States, throughout Australia and Canada, people take time each year to celebrate St. Patrick's Day. While many people think of shamrocks and leprechauns when March rolls around, there is much more to the story of the green holiday. St. Patrick's Day is a time for people to celebrate the rich heritage, history, and customs that the Irish have shared with the world.

No matter where a person is on that special day in March, there is no doubt that there will be a parade, a host of shamrocks, and a wealth of Irish spirit someplace nearby. March 17 truly is a special day: St. Patrick's Day.

Try These Tricky Steps!

Irish step dancing is a highly competitive sport, so don't get discouraged when these steps seem a bit difficult. First, stand straight, with your arms stiff at your sides, like a soldier standing at attention. Next, tuck your right knee behind your left by sliding one leg behind the other. You are now ready to learn the Jump Three step. Lift your right leg straight out and, at the same time, jump up off of your left foot. As you jump, bring your right leg up and kick yourself in the bottom. Switch legs and repeat! With a little practice, you'll be stepping just like an Irish dancer.

GLOSSARY

bishop—A Catholic Church official ranking above a priest.

blight—A disease of plants resulting in withering and death.

ceili—Irish celebration involving music, dance, and food.

Celts—Group of early Indo-European peoples living in the British Isles.

Christianity—The religion centered on Jesus Christ and the Bible.

Druids—Ancient Celtic priests thought of as magicians and wizards.

emigrants—A person parting from a country to settle someplace else.

fast—To refrain from eating food, often in the name of religion.

genocide—The systematic destruction of a group of people.

immigrant—A person who enters a country with the intention of taking up residence.

kilt—A knee-length pleated skirt most often worn by men of Scottish decent.

mass—A Catholic religious service or celebration.

mortality—The number of deaths in a given place or time.

ordination—A ceremony to declare a person as priest or other official of the church.

parasite—An organism living in or on another organism, bringing harm to the host organism.

performance artists—Artists who convey their art to an audience through actions.

politician—A person actively engaged in the business of government.

priest—A person authorized to lead religious ceremonies.

saint—A person officially recognized as being an exceptionally holy person.

shamrock—A three-leafed herb used as a symbol representing the Irish culture.

tenement—A house or dwelling meeting minimum standards for sanitation, safety, and comfort.

Trinity—The unity of Father, Son, and Holy Spirit into one absolute God.

CHAPTER NOTES

♦ **Chapter 1.** **St. Patrick's Miracles**

1. Whitley Stokes, *On the Life of St. Patrick (Leabhar Breac)* (Cork, Ireland: Corpus of Electronic Texts, 2000), p. 7.
2. Brian De Breffny, *In the Steps of St. Patrick* (New York: Thames and Hudson, Inc., 1982), p. 72.
3. Stokes, p. 7.
4. Ibid.
5. De Breffny, pp. 105–156.
6. Alannah Hopkin, *The Living Legend of St. Patrick* (New York: St. Martin's Press, 1989), p. 180.

♦ **Chapter 2.** **The History of St. Patrick's Day**

1. Mike Cronin and Daryl Adair, *The Wearing of the Green* (New York: Routledge, 2002), pp. xxvii, xxviii.
2. Brian De Breffny, *In the Steps of St. Patrick* (New York: Thames and Hudson, 1982), p. 13.
3. Ibid., p. 23.
4. Cronin and Adair, p. xxvii.
5. Saint Patrick, "Confessio of Saint Patrick," as printed in Breffny, *In the Steps of St. Patrick*, p. 155.
6. Ibid.
7. DeBreffny, pp. 155–156.
8. Ibid.
9. Ibid.
10. Ibid.

11. Ibid.
12. William J. Courtenay, "Saint Patrick," *World Book Encyclopedia*, version 6.0, (Chicago: 2002).
13. "Frequently Questions about St. Patrick," *St. Patrick's Day Parade*, n.d., <http://www.chicago stpatsparade.com/history_sp1.shtml> (August 4, 2004).
14. Christopher McIntosh, "Druids," *World Book Encyclopedia*, version 6.0, (Chicago, IL: World Book, Inc., 2002).
15. Philip Shallcrass, "A Little History of Druidry," n.d., <www.druidnetwork.org/articles/philipshallcrass .html> (March 13, 2006).
16. Ibid., p. 20
17. Ibid., p. 19
18. Ibid., p.40
19. Ibid.
20. Jack Santino, *All Around The Year: Holidays and Celebrations in American Life*, (Chicago: University of Illinois Press, 1994), p. 80.
21. Ibid.
22. Cronin and Adair, p. 1.
23. Ibid., p. 4.
24. Ibid.
25. Ibid., p. xxviii.
25. Lelia Ruckenstein and James A. O'Malley, *Everything Irish* (New York: Random House Publishing Group, 2003), p. 121.
26. Jacqualine O'Brien and Peter Harbison, *Ancient Ireland From Prehistory to the Middle Ages* (New York: Oxford University Press, 1996), p. 142
27. Ibid.
28. Ibid.

29. Ibid.
30. Ruckenstein and O'Malley, p. 121.
31. O'Brien and Harbison, p. 142.
32. Ruckenstein and O'Malley, p. 121.
33. Ibid., p. xxviii.

◆ Chapter 3. The Cultural Significance of St. Patrick's Day

1. Ciaran Brady, *The Encyclopedia of Ireland* (New York: Oxford University Press, 2000), p. 136.
2. Ibid.
3. Ibid.
4. Ibid.
5. "The Times," *University of Virginia Information, Technology and Communication*, n.d., <http://www.people.virginia.edu/~eas5e/Irish/Skibbereen.html> (September 27, 2004).
6. Mary Johnston, "Irish Emigration," September 28, 1999, <http://www.gober.net/victorian/reports/irish2.html> (October 4, 2004).
7. R.F. Foster, *The Oxford Illustrated History of Ireland* (New York: Oxford University Press, 1989), p. 56.
8. Ibid. p. 57.
9. Ibid. p. 57.
10. Ibid. p. 59.
11. Ibid. p. 59.
12. Ibid. p. 60.
13. Author unknown, "The Times: Apprehended Disturbances, March 27, 1846," *University of Virginia Information, Technology and Communication*, n.d., <http://www.people.virginia.edu/~eas5e/Irish/Disturbances.html> (September 27, 2004).

14. Mike Cronin and Daryl Adair, *The Wearing of the Green* (New York: Routledge, 2002), p. 29.

15. Ibid., p. 30.

16. Ibid.

17. Lelia Ruckenstein and James A. O'Malley, *Everything Irish* (New York: Ballantine Books, 2003), p. 132.

18. Wesley Johnston, "Effects of the Famine 2: Emigration," n.d., <http:/www.wesleyjohnston.com/users/Ireland/past/famine/emigration.html> (October 4, 2004).

19. Ibid.

20. Ibid.

21. Jim Kinsella, "Irish Immigrants in America during the 19th Century," April 2004, <http://kinsella.org/history/histira.htm> (September 17, 2004).

22. Alannah Hopkin, *The Living Legend of St. Patrick* (New York: St Martin's Press, 1989), p. 141.

23. Mary Johnston, "Irish Emigration."

24. Brady, p. 126. "Irish Emigrating."

25. Mary Johnston, "Irish Emigration."

26. Ibid.

27. Cronin and Adair, p. 34.

28. Brady, p. 127.

29. Ibid.

30. "Kate Kennedy: San Francisco's Labor-Loving School Teacher and Principal," n.d., <http://www.cooperativeindividualism.org/georgists_kennedy-kate.html> (March 13, 2006).

31. "Kate Kennedy" n.d., <http://www.uissf.org/journal/katekennedy.html> (March 13, 2006).

◆ **Chapter 4. Who Celebrates St. Patrick's Day?**

1. "St. Patrick's Day: The Story of an American Celebration," March 2004 (Chicago Public Library), <www.chipublib.org/shamrock/stpatscelebrate. html> (January 16, 2005).

2. James Akin, "All About Lent," *Nazareth Resource Library*, n.d., <www.cin.org/users/james/files/lent. htm> (January 16, 2005).

3. "St. Patrick's Day: The Story of an American Celebration."

4. Bridget Haggerty, "Celebrating St. Patrick's Day in Old Ireland," n.d., <http://www.emigrant.ie/article. asp?iCategoryID=189&ArticleID=14406> (November 15, 2004).

5. Mary Moylan, "St. Patrick's Day: Then and Now," n.d., <www.emigrant.ie/article.asp?iCategoryID= 189&ArticleID=28090> (November 15, 2004).

6. Food Services of America, "St. Patrick's Day Menu," n.d., <http://www.fasafood.com/fsacom/News+and +Information/Solutions/Menuing/St+Patrick's> (January 16, 2005).

7. Bridget Haggerty, "Celebrating St. Patrick's Day in Old Ireland."

8. "St. Patrick's Day: The Story of an American Celebration."

9. Chicago Public Library. "St. Patrick's Day," n.d., <http://www.chipublib.org/shamrock/stpats celebrate.html> March 13, 2006.

10. Ibid.

11. President George W. Bush, "Irish-American Heritage Month," *Celebrating Irish-American Heritage Month,*

n.d., <http://www.emigrant.ie/article.asp?iCategory ID=189&iArticleID=28135> (November 15, 2004).

12. Jack Santino, *All Around the Year: Holidays and Celebrations in American Life* (Chicago: University of Illinois Press), 1994. p. 83.

13. Mike Cronin and Daryl Adair, *The Wearing of the Green* (New York: Routledge, 2002), p. 38.

14. Ibid, p. 205.

15. John Wright, "St. Patrick's Day Down Under," *St. Patrick's Day*, n.d., <http://www.emigrant.ie/ article.asp?iCategoryID=189&iArticleID=28291> (November 15, 2004).

◆ Chapter 5. Symbols of St. Patrick's Day

1. "The History of St. Patrick's Day: History of the Holiday," *The History Channel*, n.d., <http://history channel.com/exhibits/stpatricksday/history/snake .html> (July 26, 2004).

2. "Shamrock," *Microsoft Encarta Online Encyclopedia*, 2004, <http://encarta.com/text_761575417_0/ Shamrock.html> (September 20, 2004).

3. Alannah Hopkin, *The Living Legend of St. Patrick* (New York: St. Martin's Press, 1990), p. 117.

4. Ibid., p. 109.

5. "A Timeline of Irish History," *Fianna Guide to Irish Geneology*, March 2002, <http://www.rootsweb. com/~fianna/history/> (March 14, 2006).

6. Mike Cronin and Daryl Adair, *The Wearing of the Green* (New York: Routledge, 2002), p. xiii.

7. Historychannel.com, July 26, 2004.

8. Micha F. Lidemans, "Leprechaun," *Enyclopedi. Of Mythica*, April 1999, <http://www.pantheon.org/ articles/1/leprechaun.html> (January 3, 2005).

9. Ciaran Brady, *The Encyclopedia of Ireland* (New York: Oxford University Press, 2000), p. 213.

10. Ibid.

11. "The History of St. Patrick's Day," *The History Channel.*

12. Brady, p. 246.

13. "Irish Dance: The History of Irish Dance," *Ireland's Eye.com*, n.d., <http://www.irelandseye.com/dance.html> (January 7, 2005).

14. Ibid.

15. Ibid.

16. Ibid.

17. Ibid.

18. Ibid.

19. "History of Irish Dance" *Ireland's Dance*," n.d., <www.irelandsdance.com/info/history/irishdance.htm> (January 7, 2005).

20. Ibid.

21. "Irish Dance: The History of Irish Dance," *Ireland's Eye.com.*

22. Ibid.

23. Alannah Hopkin, p. 81.

24. "Drowning the Shamrock," February 28, 2000, <http://www.esatclear.ie/~stfanahans/folklore_calendar.htm> (March 14, 2006).

◆ **Chapter 6.** How St. Patrick's Day Is Celebrated Today

1. Bridget Haggerty, "St. Patrick's Day Around the World," *Irish Culture and Customs*, 2003, <www.irishcultureandcustoms.com/ACalend/StPatWorld03.html>(January 13, 2005).

2. Borgna Brunner, "St. Patrick's Day: More Dallas than Dublin," n.d., <http://print.factmonster.com/spot/stpatkids1.html> (November 1, 2004).

3. Mike Cronin and Daryl Adair, *The Wearing of the Green* (New York: Routledge, 2002), pp. 184–185.

4. Ibid., p. 186.

5. Ibid., p. 187.

6. Brunner, "St. Patrick's Day: More Dallas than Dublin."

7. "St Patrick's Day Festival," *St. Patrick's Day Festival Events*, n.d., <http://www.stpatricksday.ie/cms/events_review2004.html> (November 1, 2004).

8. "St. Patrick's Festival: St. Patrick's Day Symposium," <www.stpatricksday.ie/cms/events_symposium.html> (November 1, 2004).

9. "St. Patrick's Day Festival," <www.stpatricksday.ie/cms/events_review2004.html> (November 1, 2004).

10. "St. Patrick's Day Festival: Treasure Hunt," <www.stpatricksday.ie/cms/events-treasurehunt.html> (January 4, 2005).

11. Ibid.

12. Ibid.

13. Ibid.

14. Brunner, "St. Patrick's Day: More Dallas than Dublin."

15. "St. Patrick's Day," *MSN Encarta*, n.d., <http://encarta.msn.com/text_681500369__0/Saint_Patrick's_Day.html> (September 20, 2004).

16. Alannah Hopkin, *The Living Legend of St. Patrick* (New York: St. Martin's Press, 1989), p. 135.

17. "St. Patrick's Day," *MSN Encarta*.

18. "St. Patrick's Day in New York," *New York.com*, n.d., <http://www.ny.com/holiday/stpatricks/> (January 13, 2005).

19. Ibid.

20. "Seattle's Irish Week 2005," *Seattle's Irish Heritage Club*, n.d., <http://www.irishclub.org/irwk.htm> (January 13, 2005).

21. "The Grand Parade," *St. Patrick Society*, n.d., <http://www.stpatsqc.com/GrandParade.htm> (January 13, 2005).

22. Noreen Bowden, "St. Patrick's Day: More Than Green Beer," *Emigrant Online*, n.d., <www.emigrant.ie/article.asp?iCategoryID=189&iArticleID=1462>, (November 11, 2004).

23. Ibid.

24. Dan Lydon, "The Man Who Dyed the River Green," *Chicago's St. Patrick's Day Parade*, n.d., <http://www.chicagostpatsparade.com/history_01.shtml> (August 4, 2004).

25. Nikki Usher, "Loss Adds Somber Note to Pipers' Celebration; Only Death Could Keep Bagpiper Barbara O'Hara from the St. Patrick's Day Parade," *Chicago Tribune*, http://pqasb.pqarchiver.com/chicagotribune/doc/578212501.html?MAC=8decddff63ee908d... (August 4, 2004).

26. Ibid.

27. Ibid.

28. June Sawyers, "A Big Parade, an Old Tradition Irish March Got Its Start in the 1840s," *Chicago Tribune*, 1990, <http://pqasb.pqarchiver.com/chicagotribune/doc/28848367.html?MAC=9899bd8cb3a52dff3...> (August 4, 2004).

FURTHER READING

Books

Barth, Edna. *Shamrocks, Harps, and Shillelaghs: The Story of the St. Patrick's Day Symbols.* New York: Clarion Books, 2001.

Cronin, Mike, and Daryl Adair. *The Wearing of the Green: A History of St. Patrick's Day.* New York: Routledge, 2002.

Dolan, Edward F. *The Irish Potato Famine: The Story of Irish-American Immigration.* New York: Benchmark Books, 2003.

Krull, Kathleen. *A Pot o' Gold: A Treasury of Irish Stories, Poetry, Folklore, and (of course) Blarney.* New York: Hyperion Books For Children, 2004.

Levy, Patricia. *Ireland.* New York: Benchmark Books, 2005.

Lyons, Mary E. *Feed the Children First: Irish Memories of the Great Hunger.* New York: Atheneum Books for Young Readers, 2002.

Internet Addresses

The History of St. Patrick's Day
<http://www.historychannel.com/exhibits/stpatricksday/main.html>
Learn more about St. Patrick at this Web site.

St. Patrick's Day Holiday Fun
<http://www.kidsdomain.com/holiday/patrick/>
Find crafts and other information on this Web site.

INDEX